Creativity Over Capital

HOW PROFESSIONAL REAL ESTATE
INVESTORS CREATE FINANCIAL
SUCCESS USING OTHER PEOPLE'S
MONEY.

Nico Sanchez

Couronne Publishing
WINNPEG, MANITOBA

Couronne Publishing Inc.
3377 Pembina Highway,
Winnipeg, Manitoba Canada
R3V1A2
www.couronnepublishing.com
support@couronnepublishing.com

Ordering Information:
Quantity sales. Special discounts are available on quantity purchases by corporations, associations, and others. For details,
contact the "Special Sales Department" at the address above.

Creativity Over Capital/ Nico Sanchez. —1st ed.
ISBN 978-1-988497-03-7

Contents

This book is dedicated to my family.

To my daughter, Luna. You mean the world to me. The moment you emerged into this world was the first time I ever experienced tears of joy and because of you I now know the true meaning of that phrase. You brought a new hope in my life, a new fire in my heart, and have given me a motivation to succeed without parallel. Thank you for bringing sunshine to my days with your warm, beautiful smile! Love you so much – Dad.

To my wife, Vivian. You have stuck with me through thick and thin, through good times and bad times, through financially comfortable times and times when we have been so broke that we had to pinch every penny and go on the "cup noodle diet." You understand me better than anyone else on this world. Thank you for the love and support you have given and will always continue to give me and thank you for the peace you have brought into my life. I love you!

To my mother, Jocelyn. Thank you for raising me with love, compassion, selflessness, righteousness and virtue. Without your love and support throughout my life's ups and downs, none of this would have been possible. Although I did not end up becoming a doctor like you had hoped, thank you for always believing in me with everything that I chose to do in my life! Thanks mom, I love you!

Last but not least, I thank God for providing me with love, hope, guidance and direction. It is only by HIS will that everything has been possible. I pray for humility, for whatever the Lord provides with ease can be just as easily taken away should HE will. Thus, I pray that everything that I do and achieve can and will be used to fulfill HIS plans and glorify HIS name. Amen.

As a special bonus for readers of this book, I'm offering you access to some valuable resources and templates. These Resources will come in handy in your journey to creating wealth through real estate You'll find out how you can gain access at the conclusion of this book absolutely FREE

Foreword

First off, you have made a great choice for adding this publication, Creativity Over Capital to your library. This publication is a result of years upon years of practical implementation in the real estate marketplace. I can attest to this, having personally witnessed the tips, tools, and training paving the way for success with regard to the author and those who have learned directly from the author.

This book has the potential to break down any and all perceived barriers you may have put up in your own mind about the business of real estate. This compelling guide for professional success involving real estate investments gives one of the best step-by-step systems I have ever come across.

Real estate investing is one of the fastest growing industries in the world today, and the fact that Mr. Sanchez has packaged his closely held secrets to readers is a testament to his qualities as a leader and a mentor. Having verified many accounts of proven success stories due to the author's extraordinary ability to teach those around him, I can honestly say that your identity will transform for the better after the conclusion of this book.

The successful real estate investors around the world today all reach the same conclusion about how they obtained high levels or prosperity; they will say it was because of access to specialized information and the utilization of such useful data. It is based on this premise that what is contained in this book should be deemed as nothing short of life changing.

After reading this book, I became intrigued by the valuable synthesis of information and how it was intertwined with interesting narratives. The presentation is both intensive and thrilling. The literary process you will go through, as the reader will act as a money map from zero to millions made in real estate.

This can be your reality, as it has for the author, if you simply take every word seriously and act on the proven concepts in this book. I encourage you to challenge the status quo en route to becoming a successful real estate investor and use the creative tactics to magnetize endless streams of capital for your current or would be business.

Your wish is your command in this scenario and let this book be your chaperon to unlock the richness you always dreamed of in the commerce of real estate!

Valen Vergara

President,

Team Made Real Estate Inc.

Someone Else's Money

Getting started in real estate seems simple enough. Experts on the subject have information readily available to those wanting to learn. In the digital world, the way we get information has changed rapidly. It is no longer the information age as knowledge and expertise is widely available. With access to up to date and relevant technical information available at the touch of a screen; people are able to acquire new skills rapidly. Now for those of you who want to follow a path to a more free lifestyle, it is how you use these skills that counts. There is an abundance of information online and in books on how to get started in real estate and many of you reading this have already spent time and money on training. Implementing these investment techniques and other practical advice that goes beyond getting started will give you what you need to find a deal. So where does this book fit in?

So many people have the knowledge, but feel stuck. Maybe they've read Rich Dad, Poor Dad or other books on the topic. Or perhaps they have taken a course and know real estate is the key but do not know where or how to get started. Often people will find themselves in either one of two scenarios; they do not have the money they think they need to complete a deal, or they are unsure how to go about finding the money when they find a great deal. This book will show you numerous methods to get started, including getting started without using any of your own money.

As we go forward, it will become clear that even with zero credit or zero cash, there are methods available to help you begin your real estate investment strategy. If your question is, where do I actually start? This book will provide all the motivation, including a step-by-step guide, describing everything needed for how to begin. Know that there is more than one way to move forward. By reading this book, you will discover what tactics work and the situations you might want to implement for each individual scenario. If you tried the basics, the way it is usually done and it didn't work, do not give up. There are so many ways that you can do it. It's just a matter of figuring out other options.

Once you have the knowledge, it is time to take action. The important thing is not to let the fear hold you back. Use knowledge and understanding to overcome the fear and move forward using the steps laid out in the following chapters. What I really want to drive home is that you have to take action in order to succeed. The goal here is to help you to become confident enough so that you know enough and are ready to get a deal going in real estate. Aside from the technical acquisition techniques, which is something that takes some practice and is best gained by working with a mentor, the other option is learning through trial and error which can be personally and financially painful. However, in terms of expert advice, and knowing the techniques, finding out what's possible, and what creative financial opportunities might fit; this book will help you be ready to move when the right deal comes along. Having a variety of different strategies that can be employed to be able to complete a real estate deal, offers a kick start of confidence to a new investor.

Starting off with a mindset of success will boost the outcome of your potential deals. Understanding the importance of creativity over capital requires knowledge, diligence and foresight to commit to what it takes. A lot of times when people lack the knowledge, they don't take action or recognize a potentially beneficial deal. Also, because they lack the knowledge, they're going to lack the confidence. The end result is they won't go forward with anything.

So, just when starting out, somebody might be trying to get a real estate deal going, watching what is available and trying to buy a property, eventually making an offer when the timing is right. Not knowing what comes next, all of a sudden, they might get scared and then they'll maybe back out of the deal, probably even losing their deposit. Not sure how to manage every step of the deal can be overwhelming without an intentional plan in place. A person can have the information available to get started but then who's to say what lies beyond having their offer accepted. The fear of the unknown can prevent successful deals and hold back competent investors.

Once the different financial strategies are laid out, it becomes clear what's coming next and exactly what can be done. Then the confidence to be able to go out and actually do it increases substantially. In some cases, potential investors may not have good credit, and they know they don't have good credit, but they have a little bit of cash in the bank. The traditional way of financing scares people off and they do not even try to get preapproved. In fear of have their credit score lowered even further, they give up hope of entering the real estate market.

Through the steps laid out in this book, the intention is that fear will be removed and replaced with a confident understanding. The strategies listed will show how to accomplish real estate deals that are a win/win for both parties. When we are done here, you will be able to finally have the confidence and the exact preparation required to acquire a piece of real estate and begin to build your portfolio. As well, you can find bonus tips, templates and resources to improve. Most importantly is the certainty and understanding to do a deal, creatively.

Let's get started then so you can get your creative juices flowing into the deal that is right for you. Don't allow the fear to hold you back. It is an interesting realization that the fear exists because of a lack of the proper skill set and resources to creatively finance a project. Overcome that lack of knowledge by understanding specific ways to fund your investments, and you'll overcome any fear of real estate investing. Once you overcome that fear, you can then take action, because you have the information and tools to do so. Be bold and find that creativity trumps capital every time. You have to take action in order to succeed.

With numerous methods to consider while you delve into the real estate market in your area, this book is about creating a win/win for everyone involved. The key is to use creative solutions to purchasing decisions, even getting started without your own money. It is about understanding the intricacies of the industry and solving a lot of people's problems. Anything you do in life should be a win/win scenario, and that way you are creating a better world for yourself and those around you. That's the ethical way of doing things, and it is best to keep that in mind in your real estate endeavors. A good deal is one in which everybody wins. There's so much value and wealth out there for everybody. You don't need somebody else to lose, just for you to win. Everybody can win. It's just as simple as creativity over capital.

CHAPTER 1

Why Real Estate

Having a financial mindset can sometimes color the way that investments are viewed. Traditionally, money is saved in locked-in systems that are difficult to access and do little to benefit the person as an individual on an on-going basis. As well, stock market and other investment opportunities can be exceptionally volatile with little gains over a long period of time. We really need to get out of the traditional way of thinking that's been taught to us by the education system, our family, and our peers. It would be wise to take a closer look at the implications of the financial advice taught by the school system, the government and society in general. The thought that you've got to go to school, get good grades, graduate, get a nice, stable job and then save a certain amount of whatever you make per year, and then you can retire is an archaic and often unrealistic expectation.

It is often not possible to rely on savings or company pension plans anymore for retirement funds. Money doesn't work the same way that it used to anymore. Society doesn't work in the same way that it used to work anymore either. Many people are finding they are no longer satisfied with saving until someday, they want someday right now. They want to do things a little differently. But the school system is archaic so there are huge gaps in the way the world looks, compared to the way we are taught it looks. Does the world right now look like it's the 30s or 50s? No, so even the education system is outdated and no longer providing accurate information. Yet that is the exact system we are using to learn about financial investments. Not anymore!

We need to get out of that traditional mindset of saving for our retirement, because savers are losers now. There's no gold standard. Money can be printed by the government at will. If you're saving, you're actually losing money, so savers are actually losers, literally. If you're just saving money in a bank account, you're losing money in inflation, which currently has a rate of about 3% a year.

Unless you're putting funds into some sort of account where you're guaranteed to get at least 3% in interest gains, each year, you're actually losing 3% of your wealth per year. Saving will never allow you to become rich. And other investment portfolios are even more volatile. Real estate makes sense because it offers a way to move money, often without using any of your own.

We have to keep money moving in order for it to keep growing. Think of money as a muscle. You go to the gym to build muscle and keep fir. If you just lay in bed and you don't move your muscles at all, what happens is they atrophy. So, your muscle will actually continue to shrink unless you take preventative action. It won't even stay the same, it'll actually shrivel away; the less you move, the smaller your muscle will get. It's the same thing with money. From a financial standpoint, inflation has the exact same result as atrophy. If you don't move your money, you are shrinking your bank account bit by bit through the cost of inflation. You need to keep your money moving and constantly working for you. You need to keep it going from investment to investment. It has to keep being moved about. How we're going to do that is by investing it. Think of the real estate market as your financial gym.

This is not to say that it is not possible to have other investments. You can invest in RRSPs or, you can invest in mutual funds and stuff like that. That technically is keeping your money moving. Hopefully any company pension plans or other investments are going to give you some sort of return, but it's not the return that you want. Real estate is really where we're going to get a much more favorable result, because it gives you the highest yield. I have personally had investments making an average annual return of 15% and more, and that's just from the cash flow not to mention the mortgage pay down and market appreciation!

With investments in real estate the income earning options become close to endless. The direct benefit is the one you get from cash flow. You also get it from equity build-up, or equity pay-down; which is the mortgage being paid down. That's not to mention the income advancements from appreciation, as well as tax advantages. There are four different ways your wealth is accelerating. In one year of a single investment, for the most part you're getting at least 30% of the return, on average including mortgage paydown and appreciation. That's where we want to move our money, by finding the right deals in real estate. Don't get me wrong, not every deal is going to be a home run, but it's a heck of a lot better than

3-5% returns in traditional investments don't you think?

As soon as we understand that saving keeps our investments stagnant, it becomes clear that is the same as losing. There are too many ways to use that money and watch it grow. As soon as we understand that we have to keep our money moving, we will put it in investments that result in positive gains. Once we have gained insight into the momentum required from investments, we now have to understand how money works. We have to understand that not all debt is bad debt. A car debt, that's bad debt because it's not putting money in your pocket. Real estate is considered good debt because it results in returns much greater than what is owed for the property. Often this can add up to 10 or more times as much.

To put it into perspective, the lucrative deals are done when the people involved have mutually bene-ficial interests in the property. A real estate invest-ment, is a good debt and positive cash flows are the end result. It is a given that the deal has been invested in properly and the property has been analyzed from all angles well enough that you're getting positive cash flow with very limited risks, so it's actually a good investment.

The reason it is considered good debt is because you're getting more in return for the debt that you're incurring. Whereas bad debt, ends up costing you. And to put it in the same perspective of just real estate, most people think your personal home is an asset, but it's not. You're living in it. Here's why. In more than 90% of the cases, it is not giving you a cash flow in return. In all likelihood, it is costing you more money or time than you realize. If you are still not convinced ask yourself this. When, if ever will you see a return on your personal home as an investment? Is it giving you positive cash flow in return, every single month? No, you're actually paying out for your personal home. If it's putting money in your pocket, it's good debt. If it's taking money out of your pocket, it's bad debt.

Another example of bad debt is acquiring vehicles. With $200,000 sure I could buy a Lamborghini for my garage. That would be pretty great, wouldn't it? But with the same $200,000 I could use LEVERAGE and purchase an apartment building worth $1,000,000 and that building would MAKE me money every month, every year for years to come!

Now I'm not saying that you should never spend on luxury goods and experiences to enjoy your wealth and success, it's simply a comparison of what the same $200,000 can be used for differently. In fact, I absolutely believe that you should enjoy your success! Otherwise what's the point? Life is too short to not enjoy it! I am a huge advocate in rewarding yourself whenever you make an achievement. Even small rewards are a positive way to celebrate every small achievement you make. This provides a positive feedback loop in our brain, and it releases chemicals in our bodies that give us happiness and more motivation to keep going!

I like those luxury cars, but personally I enjoy travelling and experiencing different cultures and their wide variety of foods. In fact, for the past couple of years I have been travelling over 5 months per year. This year I will be out of the country for the last 6 months of the year (I love my city, but I do enjoy escaping the winters here) Travelling with my family is how I treat myself. So, go ahead and treat yourself too. But don't do it too early. I will give you an example of how I work things when I want to purchase a new liability such as a new car.

If I want to buy a new car and the payment comes up to $1000 per month, I will first purchase an asset / investment property that will generate $1000+ in cash flow. That way when I do buy that car, it's essentially a FREE car. If my investment earns me $1200 per month in cashflow I'm basically getting paid $200 to buy that car. Not to mention the tax advantages I would get from purchasing or leasing that car under my business! Now how awesome is that?

The point is not to avoid buying liabilities entirely. Because things like a new car, or a boat, or even your personal home makes us happy even though they are liabilities. But the point is that if you want to be rich, you need to think like the rich. Always have more assets than liabilities.

A big misconception that is believed and encouraged by mainstream society when it comes to investments is that people can live in the same house for 30 years and retire off of it. Unfortunately, it is not going to happen. Many different situations can change future events and you are better off setting yourself up an investment that pays monthly rather than every three decades. Too much can happen in the meanwhile and it is a much more beneficial situation to have multiple properties paying for your expenses and then some.

If you already understand that you are definitely ahead of the game, likely that's why you are looking at all your options. That's why you are reading this book. It could be, as is common, that one of the reasons you are interested in real estate, is because of a lack of satisfaction with the current returns people are getting in their mutual funds. In a time when negative returns have been normal and in recent years where people have lost most of their investments in the money market, real estate is becoming a tangible option with multiple ways of getting involved.

Going forward, each chapter will dive into greater detail about exactly what you need to do for each specific circumstance. As a new investor, what are some of the small steps that need to be taken to begin the process; to overcome any last hesitation. These are things you can start doing right now, to take action and take advantage of the unique opportunities real estate investment provides.

CHAPTER 2

Understanding Leverage

The goal with real estate investing for most people is not necessarily to become an overnight millionaire. Instead, the key to successful real estate investing often depends on the ability to educate yourself so that you can then utilize leverage that creates cash flow, and ultimately, financial freedom.

Now people have all different reasons for investing but the expected result always ends up being the same; the return or potential gains available are the measure of success. Usually though once you begin your real estate education and training, everyone has a different perspective of how it will work for them.

In the same regard, we all have our own measure of success and how we envision our involvement. It might be the case that you have some cash set aside in a savings accounts, and you're starting to wonder what you should do with it. Should you simply leave it in the savings account and enjoy the security of knowing it's there?

When you leave a substantial sum of money sitting in a savings account, it's not growing in value because of the negligible interest rates on savings accounts, but in actuality it is losing value. In this way savings accounts are one of the riskiest investment strategies you can take with your money. For example, at the end of 2016, the annual inflation rate was just over 2%. This means that if you were to leave your money in a savings account that earns an annual interest rate of 1%, you're losing 1% of your money's value each year. If inflation goes up, which is entirely possible, you lose even more.

Once you realize the very real downside of sitting on your cash and doing nothing with it, you might start to consider the stock market. Investing in the stock market can be one of the simplest ways to put your money to work, particularly if you choose low-cost ETFs and mutual funds. So, this sounds like a good plan, right? Unfortunately, it's not the optimal investment strategy, particularly if your goals are to build not only substantial wealth but also create financial freedom for yourself.

At the same time, many of us worked hard for the amount we have and want to see it invested well. Returns on investment must be calculated to provide the results and pave the way for future endeavors. We want our money to work for us or better yet…have other people's money work for us and them because as you will see later, it is ALWAYS a win-win scenario when using private money.

The most important thing to understand so you can begin earning money through real estate investing, is the power of leverage. This works particularly well within a shorter window of time and after finding the right deal. Of course, there will be some real estate investors who will pay cash for properties, but if you don't have substantial amounts of cash simply lying around, leveraging can be a valuable way to build your real estate portfolio and investment career.

Leverage, within the context of real estate, refers to using borrowed capital to increase the returns you can achieve with an investment. With leverage, you're initially responsible only for a small down payment, and then the rest of the purchase is made by funding that comes from a third-party lender. One of the main benefits is that you aren't limited to only having your available resources to build wealth as happens when you are with the stock market. Instead, you're maximizing the use of other people's money, in this case the bank's money to then grow your own real estate portfolio and wealth. You're giving yourself more purchasing power, and that purchasing power can then be translated into higher returns.

This principal of leverage and its importance in wealth building can apply to a variety of real estate scenarios including wholesaling, buying homes to flip them, and purchasing properties to ultimately rent them and earn consistent cash flow in the process.

If you were to purchase a property as a rental using a 20% down payment, you would be seeing returns from more than one source. First of all, you will be able to just earn the monthly cash flow from that property. At the same time, you can also build equity on that property. The equity is the amount you pay on the mortgage including the interest. While your cash flow represents immediate income, the equity then represents another aspect of the asset, as it continues to grow over time. In many cases, just the equity returns alone are more than the earning potential from investing in stocks and bonds.

The power of leverage might just be the most over used and misunderstood terms in real estate. The reality is very clear, however, almost every single successful person has used the principle of leverage to drive their investment goals. In real estate, leveraging works in some unique ways because you do not have to have the entire investment amount at the outset. A real-life example might clarify the situation as to how someone can use leverage to their advantage.

One of the rental properties is a way I can show you how to maximize leverage as I did. At the time, I had met an investor and found out, through the grapevine that he was moving away. Knowing the difficulty of managing property from a distance, I had a discussion with him about it. It turned out that he had one property I was very interested in. The location was great, it was a newer house with long-term tenants who did not want to move. Now this is the kind of deal I teach people to look for. The problem was my cash flow was tied up in other endeavors and I wasn't looking for a deal at that moment. Finally, as I thought about it, I decided to use the equity in one of my other properties for the down payment and financed the rest of it. This is done by doing a "cash out refinance" or opening a "home equity line of credit" on a property that you already have equity in such as your personal home. Lenders will usually let you refinance up to 80% loan-to-value on any property.

For example, if you have a property that is worth $100,000 in today's market but you only owe a balance of $50,000 on the mortgage. Your lender can refinance 80% of the value of $100,000 which is $80,000 and you will be able to take out the balance of $30,000. You can use that $30,000 as a down payment on the next property! Did I mention that any cash you receive from a refinance is TAX-FREE? Yes, that's right, you do NOT pay any taxes on money you receive from a refinance! The same can not be said for when you cash out your RRSPs (401k). This is just one creative technique, we will get into more in the later chapters. Real estate is one of the rare investment opportunities where you can pay later and still make money on the deal now.

Leverage is an amazing tool to get you started, but there can be downsides. Although real estate almost always rebounds, there could be times when the value of your investment property decreases for multiple years in a row. In some cases, you might end up owing more than it is worth. Fortunately, rental prices do not fluctuate as much or as severely so with proper planning and a good knowledge base and network, steps can be taken to minimize the severity of the risk.

Using leverage is the secret ingredient that wealthy people implement to increase their holdings. It allows a great assortment of investment properties to be gained using other people's money.

Another attribute is the benefits in regards to taxes within the context of real estate. As was noted, when investing in stocks and bonds, tax efficiency is a challenge. Investors are usually paying either capital gains rates or their personal income tax rate on their earnings. The ability to minimize tax liability is a fundamental component of wealth building. There are many ways to reduce your tax bills in real estate investing, including depreciation, deferring profits through 1031 exchanges, and borrowing against your equity to make other investments like I did in my previous example.

Of course, this is just a broad overview of building wealth through leveraging, but it also gives an idea of why people who are wealthy have nearly always turned to real estate to get them to that point. That's not to say investing in real estate isn't without risks of course these exist. At the same time when compared to all other investment vehicles, returns on investment tend to outperform. Also, finding creative financial strategies to purchase real estate can provide the most realistic way for anyone, even beginning investors to become not just wealthy, but also create freedom for themselves. This is especially true when leveraging is used to build an investment profile.

CHAPTER 3

Money Follows the Right Deal

If you are still with me so far, you are starting to believe what I have been hinting at. The money will find you if the deal is lucrative enough. Now we are going to get into some actual techniques so we can get a little bit deeper. By sharing some personal stories and explaining how I went about it, you will learn from my mistakes and begin to see how some of these things might work in your situation.

Leveraging the bank's money and our own properties' existing equity are great but they are not the only ways to use OPM (other people's money). You can also work with other partners and investors to further scale your portfolio.

First, I want to tell you about the THREE parts of every real estate investment puzzle: 1)The Money 2)The People 3)The Deal. As well as the definition of an investor as compared to that of an entrepreneur.

The Money:

Some very good real estate deals can be TRUE $0 down deals such as a very motivated seller who is willing to do a 100% VTB (vendor take-back) with $0 down payment. We will get into what a VTB is in with more details in the later chapters but basically it is when a seller acts as the bank holding the mortgage for you and you pay them monthly. Most of the time they will ask for some sort of down payment but sometimes a very motivated seller might not require one. This is a TRUE $0 down deal. Most deals will require capital in the form of a down payment or otherwise. The beauty is that it does not have to be your money. It can be someone else's. Therefore, for you, it is still a $0 down deal.

The People:

With every investment, there is a lot of work to be done. From marketing to find opportunities, analysis of those opportunities, structuring of the deal and dealing with all the moving parts that are required to put a deal together and close on it. This is the people portion of the puzzle.

The Deal:

Of course, with every investment there must be the right deal or opportunity. Every part of this triangle is important. They must all come together for an investment to work. Now, you can play the part of all 3 by finding the deal, do all the work and use your own funds to close it. But that is not going to be a scalable business model. That is fine if you want to invest in real estate as a hobby, but not when you want to treat it as a scalable business.

If you really want to scale your real estate portfolio, you will need to learn how to work with others as a team. Be the entrepreneur. The definition of an entrepreneur in this case is someone who has the knowledge and expertise in real estate investing and can put in the time and the sweat equity that is required. Maybe you've read a lot of real estate investing books, or have taken some real estate investing programs and coaching. You know how to market for a good deal, you know how to properly analyze a deal and know all the moving parts and processes required to get that deal done.

An investor on the other hand is an individual with liquid cash that they want to grow but may not have the knowledge, the skills, the motivation or the time to do all the work required. They simply want to inject their capital into a great opportunity and reap the returns.

I think you are starting to see where this is going and how you can significantly increase your portfolio by forming great partnerships with others. The best way to get rich is by helping others get rich in the process. Teamwork makes the dream work.

Now I want to tell you a personal example story to help you understand better how this particular concept helped me scale my portfolio.

When I decided to get into real estate investing, I had a bit of capital to start out with from my home equity, savings and previous successful business venture (e-commerce). I went full steam ahead and purchased 4 properties within the first 2 months. The very first one was a 4-plex which was actually creatively acquired using a lease option. Then the other deals followed quite quickly with a duplex, a single-family house which I rented to university students by the room and then a condo which was funded by a traditional mortgage. Do you see a trend here? Because I was using my own funds and putting the properties under my own name the amount of financing I was able to get from lenders became less and less up to the point where I was unable to secure anymore mortgages and could not expand my portfolio any longer. This is the same problem that a lot of amateur investors face that causes them to stop right there and can't scale their portfolios any longer.

Now, I knew there were other ways to get around that but up until that point I just wanted to take the easiest and fastest route to acquire properties which is by self-funding them all. If I could go back in time, I would have used OPM right from the get go but I was intimidated at the thought of partnering up with other people and pitching to investors. Which is why I really want to stress to you to not let the same fear hold you back. Once I got out of that fear, it turns out it was much easier than I thought and there was really nothing to be afraid of. Everything we want is on the other side of fear, we just need to have the courage to step through it!

To continue the story, after I capped out of my own cash and credit I started to do joint ventures with other investors who would invest the cash and credit required to close on the deals that I had found, analyzed and pitched to them. Within my first year I scaled my portfolio to 29 units. It was difficult at first and I got a lot of no's from investors and joint venture partners that I pitched to, but I just kept on pushing through it and once I got a feel of what my investor partners were looking for in deals and ROI, I was able to find better deals and do better presentations which resulted in a lot more yes's.

If you're pitching an unfavourable deal to investors, guess what you're going to hear all the time? Over and over again people will tell you that they are not going to invest in what you are offering. Most times the judgement is decisive; there's no returns, and there's so much risk. In the same way, the better deals that you're getting involved in, the less risk and the more returns that other people will get, so the better chances that you are being able to secure investors for yourself. Find good deals, money will follow.

Like I mentioned before, there are some techniques that you can do by yourself even, without any investors at all. This method involves the use of home equity lines of credit, or finding other sources of credit to fund your down payments on new real estate investment. That's probably the simplest way to get money to fund your deal. And then, the more you expand your portfolio, the more equity you're going to be building in every single one of your properties. The more equity you build in the more properties, the more leverage you have now to expand. However eventually you will still run into the issue of capping out with lenders. You can only hold so many mortgages on your own before you need to start using other means to expand.

That'll really snowball the growth of your real estate portfolio, if you're doing it that way. You want to always keep your mortgages right on the brink. That is to say that, you want to always keep them at the maximum limit. You never want to have equity just sitting there doing nothing, because what's the point? If your equity is sitting there doing nothing, you can use it to acquire another property. In this way, you get more income potential, and now you have two more properties that are simultaneously building equity in both of them, and giving you positive cash flow.

Why would you ever have a property sitting there with equity, just paid down, doing nothing? That's one of my favorite ways of how to expand your real estate portfolio, is using the equity that you have, or any other source of credit that you have. Really, as long as the numbers make sense and the way that you analyze it makes sense, as long as you get paid back properly, and you're not going into a negative cash flow situation, as long as you're always in a positive cash flow situation, you're always golden.

The key to credit is all about the rate you get it at. Although it may not make sense to have credit at 30% or another rate that makes it difficult to have positive cash flow, you can always negotiate a good rate. Once you work out how to build a system that pays for itself, then you don't need the credit. However, it's good to always have the credit available in case of ever needing to use it in the future.

Simply put, it's always just good to have credit that you can use at any time, kind of just like a trump card. One example of this might be if you need to close on a deal fast and there's no time to really mess around on it. The fastest way you can close on that is using your own funds. If you don't have any liquid capital, liquid cash; you might miss out on an awesome opportunity. When you have credit, you are able to close on it quick. As long as you can turn around the investment within using equity or refinance or whatever, within the required time period, to pay back your credit cards. That way you are sure to be ready for the deal of a lifetime.

To further illustrate this point let's imagine a couple, Jack and Jill, are young and excited and just getting started and they're asking the same question that many beginner investors wonder and that is, "Hey, where do I start with getting credit?" Most commonly people go and talk to their bank, it is what we have been trained to do, even though it might not be a beneficial option. But which bank? There's really no solid answer to that and it depends on some personal criteria. It's really up to you. If you want to deal with the bank of your choice, no one can tell you which bank to deal with. Every bank and every credit card and every financial institution has different promotions for credit. They want people to open credit lines. They want people to sign up for credit cards. That's how they get their business. For financial institutions, lending is how they get their business.

They don't get their business from people just putting their money in savings, because they actually use that money, and they use it and invest it on other things. That's what a bank does. They keep their returns for themselves, and they don't give you any. You might see 0.5% return on a savings account or something like that, or 1% on a tax-free savings account. They keep the rest of the returns to themselves, to satisfy their for-profit stakeholders.

Banks want to lend out money to people, because that's how they make their money. When you're using credit cards, they're making money out of it, but you're making money out of it as well because you're using it to invest in something that's going to make you money. Now, speaking about credit, there are one or two things that allow you to use these aspects in a way that is a little different from what every other person says. There are, in some ways, trade secrets when it comes to using credit to finance a deal that most advisors won't tell you.

Seeking advice from most financial professionals, they will just tell you about the techniques that get you to buy into their products or services. Most gurus, don't really delve into the details of how certain strategies can help you and how it can hurt you. A lot of times, they only gloss over the benefits. Very few times do they ever go into details on what to watch out for or how to maximize a deal for your situation.

There are two sides to every deal and we want train ourselves to see both sides. Leverage is a double-edged sword, so unless you are using it and managing it effectively, don't use it. If you can't manage leverage effectively, don't use leverage. Stick with traditional methods of financing your mortgages or another technique described in future chapters. If you're responsible enough, and you have enough financial education and financial knowledge, then you can. There's basically two schools of thought in real estate. The first school of thought in real estate is to have everything paid off all the time before you purchase another new property. They actually go so far as to say, never buy property unless you can buy the whole thing in cash.

The other school of thought in real estate is the leveraged school of thought. The point is you never want to have a mortgage paid off. Use that equity and build and increase your portfolio even more. If you're making the right investments, then you're making sure that each deal is profitable. Each property you invest in is, you've already analyzed it, you've analyzed it to the point where, no matter what part of the market, you're not going to lose. Investors are looking for someone to do the work and find the deals.

Yes, the market does go up and down, that is not a huge secret to anyone, but you can analyze a property, and you can take that into account, the market going up and down, and you can base your strategy off of that. You still need to know how the market goes up and down. Personally, a lot of times it doesn't matter, because it always comes back around. It'll always come back up. Every eight years or so is when it happens and you take that into consideration when you are running the numbers.

Realistically, it's not only about techniques. Techniques are guidelines or maps of systems that people can take and use. We want to make sure that the knowledge and systems have helped boost your confidence so you can go find the money for your deal, because it's all about the mindset. All of these tactics are things you can be doing right now. You deal with your mindset, you can apply it right away and get results. If you don't use these tactics to move towards a mindset of success, you're probably not going to do the rest.

In your mindset, do you believe it's possible for you? If you can frame your mindset to believe, you can really focus on negotiating with people and finding value for both parties. When you do that, you are getting ready for a great deal. If you are able to negotiate with business partnerships and have a professional, confident approach, you are getting ready for great success. You need to study the deal so you understand all aspects of it. It's all in the deal.

If the deal works, it's an easy sale. In this case, stop looking for money and find a phenomenal deal that is beneficial for both parties. Money will come. Money will follow. Ask questions to figure out how to work it best. Why are you selling? What's going on? You can always negotiate. The second thing about finding the right deal is knowing your strengths and playing to them. Don't worry about the money, find a deal. If you find a deal, the money will come.

As always networking is a huge component about financing deals. You might be one of the lucky few with ample income to invest, but then you likely would not be reading a book about creative financing. So, be reassured that the deal will bring the right investment and you will be able to use your skills to make the deals happen. It is all about networking. While you may have to build momentum, you will soon see, as you have a few deals under your belt, that the money begins to find you more quickly as you begin to have success. That is when people who have more money than time might connect with you and want to work together on future deals.

When making a deal with creativity over capital in mind, negotiation is an area to spend considerable time and energy. The most important thing about negotiation is you have to know, it's still just problem-solving. Negotiation is solving problems and creating solutions that benefit both parties of the deal. If you know what the other party needs and what they're looking to get, and you know what their situation is, you can solve the other person's problem. The more information you have on the person or on the situation, the more leverage you have over it in that negotiation.

Get to know the situation. You might not learn that the homeowners are gearing up to be moving quickly. If you don't know the reason that they need to close, that they need to sell fast, then you don't have as much leverage in that negotiation. You don't have a good position in the negotiation. If I found out their reasoning and they have to make an urgent payment deadline so they need to close fast, then I would try something like this: "Listen, I know you're selling it for 150. I also know that you're eager to get that payment deadline and you need to sell this place quick. Here's what I can do for you. I can't buy it for 150. It doesn't make sense on the market. It doesn't make sense compared to similar listings. So, if you have it listed at 150, it might take a little longer than you anticipate. If you need to sell it right away, the most that I can do is 100, and I can pay you in cash in less than seven days. We'll close this thing."

How attractive do you think that scenario would look to that person? I know it's a $50,000 discount, but in this deal the need to sell and close as quickly as possible because of the situation was worth more than waiting for someone to pay a higher price. That is not to say that the owner would take that deal. But because I said I would pay cash and close in less than a week, there is a high likelihood that he'd probably take that deal. I know I would, especially if I was going through a situation like this. This just goes to show how the money follows the right deal.

Often, in creative deals like this example, the seller will come back with a counter offer, saying something like, "You know what? Sure, if we can close it in seven days, let's close it in five days, at $110,000." Now this is not far from the deal you proposed and if the property's worth is at or more than the original asking price, we still have got a good deal here. What's more important is that it is coming closer to win/win terms. Other outcomes might not be so agreeable but as always there are ways to handle it. Perhaps the seller insists, "I want a deposit right now, tonight. I want a $5,000 deposit tonight. I want you to close in five days, and I want $10,000 more."

Keeping in mind the deal and how it has worked for other people you have networked with, mentors, etc. You can keep the negotiations going with something like this: "Listen, I'll pay you the $10,000 more, I'll close in five days, and I'll close all in cash, pay all at once, but I can't give you the deposit tonight, because I don't have everything I need in writing. I'll get you the deposit tomorrow, once we have everything in writing. Does that work for you?"

The owner agrees that it works for them and perfect, boom, we've got a deal. That's a win/win scenario. That's a negotiation, and that's a perfect example of knowing what the situation is, and having information on what the seller is really looking for, what they're looking to get, what they need out of the deal, and then using all that information that you've gathered to your advantage, and you can use it as leverage for the negotiation. It's problem-solving, is all it is.

Never negotiate one way; all negotiation is two-way or it is not going to work out in a positive way. If you're solving problems there is a bigger picture than just the immediate real estate transaction. If you're thinking about the other person's needs and the other person's wants, it's a lot easier to negotiate and to combine them, because it's give and take. The law of reciprocity; if you ask me for something, you have to give me something in return. Going into a deal hoping to trick or take advantage of the other person is not ever going to work out. As well, it is just bad businesses. So, figure out beforehand where you can compromise and come up with solutions that are beneficial to all involved.

It is something that I cannot overstate, because if you have a good deal, money will follow. Money follows good deals. It's really that simple. There are people out there with money waiting to become involved in real estate but do not have the time or the knowledge to become involved. If you have a good deal, and you show it to somebody, they'll be like, "Wow, I want a piece of this deal. How do I get in on this action?" Then the ball is in your court. You can tell them that they need to invest a certain amount or whatever terms you want to set up. That's how you pitch to investors. "Listen, I have this great opportunity for you. This is what the deal looks like." Later we can go into more detail about how exactly to pitch the deal.

For now, focus on learning how to find the best deals that suit your situation. Getting creative and taking time to find the right deal is the way to take action, especially once you are committed with the confident knowledge that the right financing will be available to you. The next few chapters dive into creative investing in real estate and provide some specific ways to set up an investment strategy that maximizes your returns.

CHAPTER 4

The Art of Creative Real Estate Investing

C reative financing has been around for as long as people have been making arrangements with one another. But unlike traditional real estate transactions, creativity is favoured over cash purchases. While it is not as well-known, or even as popular, as investing your money in real estate, opportunities do exist. Sometimes it is just a case of being in the right place at the right time!

To be successful in this type of real estate investing (which as the title of the chapter suggests is indeed an art form) you are required to tap into the well of your knowledge. Deep down in some situations—forgetting what you know and being open to learning as much as possible. Over and above that, you need time and patience— whatever you have to spare.

The ability to make money from investing zero dollars does not occur overnight. Money will be required to secure these real estate deals; just not yours. If you think outside the box and imagine that your sources of finances are limitless, then it will happen. It is as simple as that! A property deal is still a deal, even if it is not your cash involved in the scheme.

Using your creativity to procure good real estate will allow you to be prosperous regardless of the weather, in good times and bad. Creative financing utilizes little-known deals with limited or no competition, feeds off motivated sellers and attempts to turn every lead into money.

As with any business deal, you must pay attention to the minute details; and most importantly, dot the I's and cross the T's. These five rules will ensure you remain focused from start to finish. Sticking to them like glue is the difference between an average investor and a highly successful one. But where do you start? Here are my top five rules of creative investing that can be applied to any potential deal.

5 Rules of Creative Investing

1. Seek the best deal possible

When investing creatively, you need to be one step ahead of everyone else, which means seeking out even better deals than those who devote their time in more traditional property opportunities. Don't jump into any deal and search for the right people to be involved in the deal. Take this example of investor A and investor B, both trying to buy up a $300,000 property which turns out to be the right market value for that certain property. Investor A is interested in the traditional route, while Investor B is a self-confessed creative investor.

Investor A: If investor A decides to take the traditional route, they will buy the home with a down payment. To keep the example simple to follow we will say 10% down. The investor is then stuck with a standard term mortgage and owes 90% loan-to-value on their home.

Investor B: As investor B is a creative investor with superior negotiation skills, he or she is tapping into their vast reserve of knowledge. They have taken the time to carry out their checks, ultimately obtaining the property for $240,000 with only 5% down payment which they got by using equity in their personal home. There is a higher profit and a superior Return on Investment (ROI) because not only did they use OPM for the down payment, but they put down 5% less and also automatically have $60,000 in equity in the new property given that the market value is $300,000.

These types of deals involve the right knowledge, skill sets and understanding how to use these specific techniques to the advantage of everyone involved.

2. Be a problem solver

By asking enough appropriate questions, you will be able to get to the crux of the issue and address it with a suitable investment deal. Change your perspective on things. Rather than attempting to acquire the best deal for you, endeavour to solve the problem of the seller by helping them move their house quickly and easily. It is a win-win for everyone. You are not trying to get one over on anybody but rather, removing obstacles and easing complicated property situations, all of which requires no capital outlay from your part. Just because they haven't thought of it, doesn't mean they aren't open to it. Be the guide, and show them the way.

Share your knowledge and seek properties where your creative financing might be of benefit to the seller. In some cases, owners no longer want the hassle of maintenance and do not require a large lump sum payment. This might be a good candidate for a lease option. Which is actually exactly how I acquired my first 4-plex. The owners were having issues managing the property to I offered to take that responsibility off their hands. At the end of the day, I put a property manager in place so that I don't personally manage the property or any of my properties for that matter. The property is now better managed. The owners are happy because they're no longer stressed from managing, the tenants are happy because the place is managed more effectively, the property manager is happy because he's getting paid, and I'm happy because I was able to get it at a steal of a deal from motivated owners and I'm making money on it too. Everybody is happy and everybody wins! Knowing the techniques will allow you to see what situation are most advantageous.

3. Always be mindful

While it does seem a little contradictory, you must be a tad conservative. You also have to be mindful of the situation, especially in terms of projections and cost analysis. Have you taken all the expenses into account including the unforeseeable and unexpected ones? Does the profit outweigh the cost? If there is no acceptable profit margin, it is not worth your time or your effort. Go through everything with a fine-tooth comb and play out the alternatives. When you have exhausted all avenues, and are still in the black, then it might be the one for you.

Look at the best-case scenario but also the worst-case scenario. What do you have to lose? If it still looks good on paper, even considering an outcome that is less desirable than you are expecting, you are likely good to go. Lowering your projections also makes for a pleasant surprise when your initial expectations come to fruition. It is like a little bonus.

4. Maintain a comfortable safety net

With every investment, comes a small amount of risk; it is not an effortless route by any stretch of the imagination. As successful entrepreneurs understand, things can and do go wrong. Earning money as an investor is not a guaranteed source of income. Despite knowing this, do not lose heart! But to be on the safe side, you do need to have a sufficient pool of money to dip into should something go awry, the size of which will be determined in Step 3. Try to keep the price as low as possible under the typical market value to reduce the risk from your point of view.

No matter how impressive a property looks there are always unexpected surprises. If not carefully accounted for, these can add up big time. Some things that might happen that you cannot plan for might be a sudden loss of rental income (sometimes an influx of availability makes the rental market tough for owners), or a major repair that went unnoticed. Foundation issues are a big one and can be missed by inspections. So, you might get the unwelcome news that your great deal of a property requires tens of thousands of dollars in renovations before it is even habitable. Knowing the risks and possible expenses is good planning and prevents unnecessary panic.

5. Hard work is necessary and good for you

One thing for certain, any sacrifice needed on your part is not based on your finances. It comes from all the blood, sweat and tears and seemingly unlimited amounts of research and calculations undertaken. As each property offers something unique, so does each transaction between yourself, the seller, and the buyer. If you assume it is going to be straightforward, then you are in for a surprise. Much of the laborious work is done behind the scenes. So for anyone else looking in, it seems like it is an easy ride.

Where you go next from here is all up to you. Your expertise will competently guide you through the negotiation, and your skills will enable you to oversee the project with minimum unexpected occur-rence. Whatever the route, your groundwork and studies will see the task through to completion.

Remember the more creative and unconventional you can be, the more ventures you will be able to swing your way. Keep your bases covered and all will go according to plan, in most cases! Absolutely, remain focused on your mindset. Before you're able to acquire knowledge, you have to have the proper mindset. If you have a negative mindset and you have a closed mind, it doesn't matter how many books you read, you're always going to shun it away. "Oh, this will never work. I've read like 100 books in real estate, it'll never work," because your mind is closed. The size of your mindset is the context and what is in your mind is the content.

Think of a cup as the context and the water inside is the content. With a closed mind, your cup is al-ready full. It has no more room for any new content or information. Your water might also be dirty, so that's your negative mindset. If you are one of the ones who notices how dirty their water is, and we have all been there, throw it out. Remove it and do not allow the negativity to creep back in. Now consciously refill your cup with positivity. The techniques in this book will fill your cup with clean water. And I hope that I can also encourage you to switch to a larger cup and expand your context by learning how to think more outside the box.

In my early years, I had this very problem and I will share a story that illustrates this in context. When I was interested in getting going in real estate, there was a course that cost more than 10 grand. My mindset was wrong, my cup was filled with dirty water, so I said "I don't have 10 grand." A month later I was in the same place and my mentor had the same conversation with me and he replied, "You don't have the confidence to find the money. It's not that you don't have money or you're poor, it's your mindset. You have a poor mindset." That pretty much stopped me in my tracks as he went on to explain that in real estate, you have to know how to raise capital. In business, you're going to have to learn how to raise capital for your business, if you want to get started and grow your business.

He told me flat out, if you don't have 10 grand, I'm sure you have family members or friends or someone somewhere that can lend you money, and you just pay them back later. Go out and raise the capital. So, I made a few phone calls to some people that owed me some money, opened up a new credit card that had a 1% interest rate for 6 months promotion and overnight, I raised the money. It just opened up my mind in a totally new way. Previously, I had closed off my mind to the possibility and left it at that. Since I did not have the cash in my hand, and I did not see how I could get the money in a traditional sense, I stopped trying. The moment that you say you can't, that's it, you're done. You'll never succeed. The moment that you say to yourself in your mind that you don't have the money, or it is not possible, you have already lost. What you should be saying is,

"How can I?" That's what you should be focusing on. Robert Kiyosaki talks about that in his books as well, explaining that instead of saying, "I can't," you should be saying, "How can I do it?"

Bringing this all back to my cup example, this is your opportunity to fill it well. Your context is the cup, and the water that you put in that cup, is the content. If it's already full with dirty water, aka the negative mindset, you'll never learn any more new knowledge. How can you get to the knowledge part if you don't even have the mindset, the context, to be able to fit more content in?

The mindset you should have is exactly what I said earlier. Instead of saying and believing that it can't be done or that it will never work, you have to get out of the negative mindset. Work towards keeping a positive mindset, and a problem-solving mindset, which is, "Okay, this didn't work because I tried it. Now, how can I make it work? There's got to be a way to make this happen." It is important to seek out this creative mindset because that's where the money is going to be found.

Getting into the creative mindset takes what doesn't work and finds a solution that is ideal for everyone. Essentially finding a way to make it work. That's the creative mindset that we want to have, and that's the creative mindset that we want to encourage. To even go a little bit further on the mindset, people might say, "How can you just change your outlook? You can't just change your mindset. You have to read books, and you have to do this, and it's hard to change your mindset because of the way that you've been born, the way that you've been taught in schools, and our peers and our family and stuff like that. We can't just change our mindset."

The truth is anyone can change their mindset at anytime. It doesn't take years to change your mindset. It doesn't take months. It doesn't take weeks. It doesn't take days to change your mindset. It takes literally less than 10 seconds to do a complete mindset change. How we do that, how we achieve that change of our mindset, is just a choice, that's it. The work is keeping ourselves in that mindset and not allowing it to revert back to negativity. Simply decide.

It's a decision, a conscious choice. It's saying, "I will no longer have this negative mindset. I will open my mind to more different creative ways, and I will change the way that I think." As soon as you make that choice and you commit to it, which takes seconds, not years or months or any length of time. It literally takes seconds for you to decide and commit on a choice of really changing the way that you think, and opening your mind and changing your mindset.

When it comes down to it, the art of creative real estate deals is in changing how you look at a deal. Get started by removing the negative mindset. So, in order for you to gain wealth, you have to have a positive mindset. Show the investors that you know a good deal when you see one and work on your professional negotiation and acquisition skills by studying those people who have skills you want to emulate and get the proper guidance and mentorship. I cannot stress enough how important having the right guidance and mentorship is and how it has helped me in my path. Know that it is up to you to be committed enough and have the passion to be involved in creative financing.

CHAPTER 5

Lease with option to buy

One of the most common questions about real estate financing is the clever ones who ask right away how to get started without an initial investment. Nothing worth having is free, right? Well, not quite. In some cases, with lease options, creative deals can be made that are mutually beneficial and require little to no down payment or financing.

A lease option is a rental agreement that includes a clause to purchase at the end of a specified time period. This type of arrangement combines elements of a traditional rental agreement with an exclusive right of first refusal option for later purchase on the home. Among other things, this allows tenants who could not qualify for a loan be able to save up for the required down payment. Giving them time to build their credit, establish a longer job history, or repair whatever is prohibiting them from obtaining a mortgage. I actually acquired my first creative deal by doing a lease option.

Less than a week after finishing my first real estate course, I saw a private advertisement for a fourplex. He had it privately listed, and that's not going through a realtor, for $120,000. I was already looking at properties and analyzing them, so I called and started building a rapport with the seller, figuring out why he was selling the property, what he was looking to get out of it. He was tired of managing the place; managing a fourplex by yourself can be a bit of a headache. So, I sent him two offers. The first offer was a cash offer of $100,000, right? The second offer was, the full $120,000; no discount if he would agree to a lease option. I explained to him that the benefit would be selling the property at the price that he wants, working on a three-year contract. At the end of the term of three years, I have the option to purchase the property, or I don't have to. If I don't purchase the property, he keeps the $5,000 deposit. It's non-refundable. If I do purchase the property, the $5,000 goes towards the purchase price, and so does all of the monthly mortgage payments over the term of the lease. This worked well and I am earning income from that property, monthly, to this day.

There are two main components of a lease option:

1. **The rental agreement or lease**: This document contains the monthly rental amount and agreement, additional fees, due dates and other information. As well, the personal information of both parties and the address of the property are included.

2. **An option to purchase**: This is a contract that provides the lessee an option to purchase the property, though they are not obligated to. In other words, a

legal document is drawn up, in which the owner offers to sell the property for a predetermined price after the initial time period determined in the agreement. All fees and terms are set out and a non-refundable deposit is included to show intent to purchase. This fee is negotiated at the time of the lease and usually costs approximately 3% of the price of the property.

Key Benefits of Lease Options

For Owners/Sellers

1. Repairs are the responsibility of the tenant. This alleviates the owner from expensive renovations and major upgrades that are often required before traditionally listing a house for sale.

2. Tenants who plan to purchase the property often take better care of it. Instead of monthly rentals, people who are renting to own, who

have invested in a lease option have good reason to keep the house in good condition.

3. Incentive for on-time payments so the tenant doesn't lose their investment. The owner is much less likely to have to chase down rent and has a more or less guaranteed monthly income.

4. No real estate agent or commission. Not having to use a middle man not only saves money but it can remove the opinion of someone whose sole interest is in selling the property.

5. Less turnover and fewer rental costs. A lease option puts in place a long-term tenant. Less turnover is less hassle, and cleaning and other costs are reduced.

6. Potential for a larger sale price. The owner is in the position of power when negotiating a lease option and can often get their asking price without reductions.

For Tenants/Buyers

1. Maximizing the appreciation value. By leasing the property, the buyer is benefiting from appreciation before purchasing it.

2. No credit, no problem. You do not have to qualify for a mortgage until you exercise your option to purchase at the end of the lease term which gives you ample time to build your credit over the term to be approved easier when the time comes.

3. Following a precise exit strategy. Lease options also allow for a specific exit strategy to be managed and controlled from the outset.

4. Buying for less, locking in a sales price. The lease option sets a sales price upon agreement of the contract. This number could go up substantially in the few years of leasing yet the buyers price is locked in.

5. Increased ROI, zero down deals possible. Lease options are some of the best ways to do a deal with zero money down, which increases ROI.

6. A home to call their own. Someone looking for a place to live will be building equity, not just paying rent when they sign a lease option.

The rental laws in each region can differ significantly and you want to always make sure that you're doing everything ethically. Sometimes owners might not consider the viability of a lease option situation and look for tenants that will not qualify for a mortgage in order to keep the deposit and continue renting. These situations are what lead to the negative image of lease option real estate deals. However, simple steps can be taken to prevent similar unfortunate situations.

Step 1: The Power Team

In real estate, a solid power team is crucial. What is a power team? These are the people that you're working with very closely and directly; your lawyer, your accountant, the closest realtors, your mortgage broker and property manager. These are people that are going to be involved in the fine points of the deal. Each one should have expertise in their aspect of the lease option deal from legal to financial, etc.

Step 2: Figure out your Finances

Guess what? After the lease is up, you still have to pay the balance owed and that usually involves qualifying for a mortgage. By figuring out your finances from the get go, you can spend that three years building your credit and saving for a down payment. Did you know that your credit can be built up in about two years? If you keep a good record of payments and transactions, in a few years, anybody would be able to purchase a property. That's why we always set our terms for three years. Speak with your mortgage broker at the outset to ensure you are on the same page. Planning in advance will ensure you do not lose out on your investment.

Step 3: Allow for Time

Make sure you leave ample time in your contract to qualify for a mortgage and have everything in place for the lease option to occur smoothly. The longer your contract is, the better. The more time you have, the more options you have. So that when it is time for payment and title transfer, all details are covered and can be completed with ease.

Step 4: Transparency

Whether you are the buyer or seller in any deal, use honest business practices. If you are going to sublet the place, do not pretend you will be living there. Be transparent in your negotiations so that both parties know what they are getting into. As a seller, screening the tenant will prevent unpleasant surprises. Always run a credit and background check and look for a stable person who is more likely to be reliable. Everyone should know local and federal tenancy and discrimination laws and connect one another to mortgage professionals and other services as required.

> Note: Never sign anything without having your lawyer go over it.

This could be a step all by itself and it cannot be understated. That way you are protected if the seller puts something in fine print that you don't understand. A good lawyer will make sure that everything is as it should be and there is nothing in the contract that will be a disadvantage.

Potential Problems with Lease Options

---

1. The Due on Sale Clause

A due-on- sale clause is a clause that stipulates that the full balance of the loan may be called due (repaid in full) upon sale or transfer of ownership of the property used to secure the note. Additionally, some mortgages forbid lease options. These circumstances are such that you might not want to pursue that specific property unless you are comfortable with the risks. Creative finance is about finding solutions, not forcing them. It would likely be best to avoid properties with this clause.

2. Major Repairs the Owner Can't Cover

Repairs can be problematic for both owner and buyer. If a lease option falls through an owner could be stuck with major repairs and no way to pay for them. As well, a buyer could quickly find some surprises that are far more expensive and complex than expected. Then they might be tempted to decline the option to purchase and lose their investment. One solution is for the concerned party to pay for a home warranty that covers these situations. At around $500, these policies can provide peace of mind.

3. Changing Legislation

In a changing real estate environment where legislation locally and federally is rapidly changing, small investors face uncertainty and risk. Be mindful and know what is acceptable in your region before agreeing to any contract.

4. Declining Real Estate Prices

This does not happen often, but it can occur. Sometimes the price of real estate in a region can drop significantly over time and be slow to recover. In this unfortunate situation, it can result in losses if a lease option was agreed to at a price higher than what the property is now worth. Hopefully though the deal was set up with no down payment or other provisions to minimize losses in this eventuality. Knowing it is possible gives you the opportunity to prepare for it.

Understanding the different types of rent to own scenarios and how they can benefit the unique situations of buyers and sellers serve to maximize the success in this endeavor. A straight lease option is the simplest form that should, in the perfect situation, be agreeable to both parties. A lease option sandwich is what happens when the investor (tenant) markets and leases the property to another tenant. The primary lessee is both a lessee and a lessor meaning the party both collects rent and pays rent.

What does a lease option sandwich look like? Once you have found a great property and made arrangements regarding a lease option with the current owner, complete the paperwork and move on to the next step. Begin looking for someone who is interested in a rent-to-own deal and sign a lease option with the new tenant. In this way, there are two lease options with you in the middle, facilitating the transaction and managing the property.

Depending on how everything works out, it might be in your best interest to simply keep the property or wait until a more advantageous time frame. The lease option is beneficial for its flexibility in that regard. By planning ahead and knowing the facts, there will be no surprises and you can use the lease option in a safe, fair and financially viable way.

The master lease option is a concept that can be tremendously attractive to those looking for creative ways to invest by leasing a property without owning it. One example might be for an apartment building; the owner receives monthly payments but is no longer involved in any aspect of the property management. The lessee manages rent collection, bill payment, maintenance and tenancy agreements; acting as the proxy owner and receiving cash flow and appreciation benefits. Since there is no change in title the risk is minimal. This can be a great way to buy a large multifamily complex using no personal money in the transaction.

Whichever option ends up fitting your scenario, there will be unexpected occurrences and learning curves to go through. Following the steps and advice listed in this chapter should be a good kick start to try out this creative financing option. In the real estate industry, there are a few things that some of us have had to learn; often the hard way. These last few tricks will hopefully keep you from experiencing the same thing.

1. **Arrange to pay the owner's mortgage for him**. That way you can avoid the unpleasant surprise of finding the bank is foreclosing on the property because the owner stopped making payments.

2. **Legally record the option contract**, so the owner will not be able to sell the property until it's cleared. Otherwise, the owner could sell to someone else with little recourse.

3. **Be respectful.** Lease option tenants may not end up purchasing the home and some owners will provide barriers to make it nearly impossible to fulfill the agreement. If both parties work towards a win-win situation, there is less likely to be difficulties. Simply put, don't be a jerk.

Instead of waiting for the whim of the financial industry, people can get into property investing without a huge down payment and waiting for approval and processing. For sellers, earning a higher sales price and terms that protect the property offer alternatives to publicly listing a property or traditional renting. As well, a transition of management might be easier on other tenants and stakeholders with a lease option that is handled efficiently between lessee and lessor. By taking the time and attention to detail to properly apply this information, lease options can become an excellent investment strategy for people looking for creative real estate financing.

CHAPTER 6

Vendor Financing

With mortgage rates jumping to a 2-year high towards the end of 2016 and experts predicting a continuous rise in the coming years, finding new and creative ways to finance your real estate endeavors has never been more important than it is today. Just as having different tools to work with can mean more building options for a carpenter, making sure you have a variety of real estate financing techniques will open up the door to even more opportunities.

In addition to increased buying power, the more financing techniques you have at your disposal, the better you'll be able to weather economic turmoil in the housing market. After all, gaining financial freedom is just as much about defense as it is about offense.

One such financing technique is vendor financing. In this chapter, we'll be discussing just what makes vendor financing such a great option for certain situations, how it differs from the lease option and why using it correctly will take (just a little) homework on your part.

What is Vendor Financing?

Also known as owner financing or seller financing, vendor financing bypasses a bank loan or a mortgage completely and instead allows the seller to loan out to the buyer directly. The vendor and buyer write up a contract according to their own terms and conditions and typically the buyer will pay an established monthly rate to the vendor, just as with a mortgage from a financial company.

The difference between vendor financing and the lease option is in regards to who holds the title to the property. In the lease option, the owner holds the property in their name, while the buyer makes payments, the title transfer is done after all money is paid. The difference in vendor financing is that the owner, the person selling the property also acts as the bank. In this case, the title transfer is done as part of the contract and the buyer has the title in their name from the outset. This has implications in regards to insurance, property tax and other costs associated with owning a property. Vendor financing is done a little bit differently and has specific advantages associated with it.

One of the biggest and most obvious benefits of going the route of vendor financing is the incredible amount of flexibility it provides you. Whereas a mortgage from institutional lenders may typically be quite rigid in its terms, vendor financing is usually a fluid and adjustable agreement that is really only constrained by the needs and wants of the buyer and seller.

Though vendor financing can be a bit rare in the world of real estate, it's used more frequently than normal in a variety of situations. If, for example, the buyer and seller know each other well and have a built up a significant amount of trust, they may choose to go the vendor financing route to speed along the process.

When the market is especially harsh and mortgage rates make traditional financing simply out of reach, you're also more likely to see a rise in this type of financing.

Vendor Financing: The Pros

The flexibility that vendor financing provides is by far the most appealing aspect. Here are a few more ways you can benefit from using this financing solution.

• **Creative Terms**: As mentioned before, the main reason for going the vendor financing route is the flexibility it provides. That means payment terms, grace periods, interest rates, and more are all up to the buyer and seller.

As such, that can allow you to even add an element of bartering to the equation, trading your own assets (e.g. personal cars, boats, vacation homes) for a reduced price altogether.

• **Lower Initial Costs**: There are other benefits the flexibility of vendor financing provides as well. Since the terms and conditions of the contract are usually between the buyer and seller alone, vendor financing can turn an everyday deal into a great one.

When the conditions are just right, that can mean a possibility of either low down payments or even none at all. It all depends on the seller and your negotiation skills.

• **Bypass the Banks**: Most lenders don't entertain mortgage options for buyers with more than four mortgages on their plate already. This can be particularly troublesome for investors and entrepreneurs looking to beef up their real estate portfolio.

Using vendor financing, on the other hand, lets you set up a structured, legally binding financing arrangement without the banks meaning no mortgage caps to deal with. It can mean a speedier process and less closing costs as well.

• **Avoid Credit Barriers**: Bypassing the banks can give you a variety of benefits when trying to finance a real estate venture and avoiding a credit check can be one of the most important. For many people, a bad credit score can be the only thing holding them back from traditional institutional financing options and, as such, they are typically left to find other means of purchasing real estate.

Depending on the seller, a credit score that might be too low for a bank could end up being just fine for the vendor. And beyond that, a lot of sellers won't even sign up with credit reporting agencies at all, meaning your credit score is less likely to be impacted.

Vendor Financing: The Cons

While vendor financing can open up a whole new world of real estate financing options, it can of course have its downsides as well.

The most notable drawback to vendor financing is the due-on-sale clause. This clause is typically included in most modern mortgages. It acts as a protection for institutional lenders in that if a lender discovers the owner of the property being mortgaged has sold it to another party, the lender has the legal right to collect payment of the mortgage in full immediately.

This, of course, can pose as quite a problem for anyone still paying off their mortgage. Tens, possibly hundreds of thousands of dollars could be due within a single month rather than within 30 years. If the owner is unable to pay off the mortgage in that time period they risk foreclosure.

The clause became almost universally used in institutional mortgages after the late 1980s. As such, anyone considering vendor financing, whether selling or buying, should simply assume the clause is included if they aren't 100% sure. If the proper precautions aren't taken, the situation can become financially devastating for both parties involved.

While there are situations where the due-on-sale clause will not apply (e.g. transfer of ownership resulting from death, transfer to spouse or children, utilizing a land trust, getting permission from the lender), the safest and simplest way of avoiding the clause is ensuring the home loan is paid off in full.

The due-on-sale clause is without a doubt the most damaging of the vendor financing drawbacks but there are a few more:

• **Title Troubles**: Transfer of the title can be problematic in vendor financing. The safest way for vendors to ensure they don't have to endure costly and time intensive litigation if the buyer defaults is an agreement for sale. This lets the seller remain titled owner until the buyer pays off the loan in full.

• **Buyer Security**: As with any agreement that goes outside widely-used terms and conditions, vendor financing doesn't necessarily give buyers the protections they might expect. A proper appraisal of the home's value, a mandatory inspection, and mortgage insurance are all not necessarily included in the contract. That means it's especially critical to read over the terms and conditions in the contract with vendor financing.

• **Availability**: While vendor financing provides a range of flexibility and a variety of negotiation options, one of the biggest drawbacks is that it may be hard to find a seller that's interested in going this route. A large number might be locked in to a mortgage with a due-on-sale clause and others may just want to keep things traditional. Either way, finding a seller open to vendor financing is typically a bit more difficult. Keep your eyes peeled in listings for the terms "for sale by owner", "FSBO", "owner will carry", and "OWC". If all else fails, just ask!

Vendor financing offers a highly flexible alternative to the rigid terms and conditions of traditional institutional real estate financing. In this situation, again it takes creativity and research to find the right property and circumstances that this technique might be most beneficial in. An owner who has the property title free and clear, in a market with rigid mortgage rules might be the perfect fit. Other times a deal might come up between two people who are acquainted. If trust is in place and a mutually explicit contract has been drawn up, great things can happen using vendor financing. And when used creatively and effectively, it can mean a substantial boost to your real estate portfolio without having to put any money down.

CHAPTER 7

Joint Venture Partnerships

Partnering with someone can power up your real estate investing potential in incredible ways. This is a strong strategy that combines networking with the power of other people's money. Using joint venture partnerships can make momentum possible at those times your cash reserves are low. If you see the opportunity to move forward with a property purchase, and the only thing holding you back is limited cash, the right partnership can help you complete the deal. As we delve deeper into this topic, you will find some hints and tricks on how to maximize this possibility.

This method of creative financing can accelerate the process of purchase, repair and resale. Those of us who become successful real estate investors rely on developing relationships with other investors because partnerships can lead to lucrative deals. Keeping an open mind and practicing professionalism in every deal will lead you to the investors who want in on your expertise.

A partner who has cash, also known as a money partner, is happy to invest alongside an entrepreneurial partner who handles the operational side. It's a common form of real estate deal, with profits typically being split 50/50 on completion. The risks and rewards of the joint venture are shared. This magic happens because one partner fulfills the wants and needs of the other and they complement each other's skill sets.

For example as the entrepreneurial partner, I have the knowledge, skills, contacts, and time to market and find good deals and opportunities, analyze and structure that deal, and create a presentable investment opportunity package to show to potential investors because of all the steps I have taken before to achieve that such as getting the proper education (which can be expensive). Having the right mentorship and guidance, being part of the right networks, and having the prior experience and track record to back it up. However, I may not have all the cash to acquire the deal and this is where the money partner comes in.

As the money partner, I have the capital but I may not have the knowledge and skill sets to do the work and research required. Or I might just not have the time. The money partners I have had the most success with were busy professionals, doctors, lawyers, or businessmen who know the value of investing in real estate but just do not have the time to learn how and do it themselves because they are busy or much rather spend their time in their own fields and just investing their capital into entrepreneurs who would do the leg work for them!

So let me get one thing straight. As the entrepreneur, you are not out there begging for capital to fund your deals. You are not asking for favors, and you are not doing people a favor. You are providing value and fulfilling a need that someone else has, and they are doing the same for you.

Reputation and respect are two values at the forefront of this strategy. Both parties must be able to offer what the other one needs. It is often necessary to build a reputation for a good eye for real estate, as well as have the respect of your network of peers.

By focusing on your strengths and personal participation it's possible to attract a money partner, someone who prefers not to do the labor of a project. If your abilities include having knowledge, being creative and having flexibility when it comes to your time—as well as being able to find and follow through on a deal—you can build a reputation as a reliable hands-on partner in real estate investments.

To attract a joint venture partner who is willing to invest capital, you must establish yourself as a brand within your community and network. So, you might not find a joint partner for your first deal. For example, as a first step you need to think about how people you interact with benefit from who you are. This aspect will be covered in more detail a bit later in this chapter. Suffice it to say for now, always keep in mind, you never know who is listening and watching you, so remain professional in every instance.

Types of Joint Venture Partnerships

As with other creative financing strategies, there are different ways a partnership deal could play out. Some of the common types of partnerships you find in real estate investment deals are detailed as follows:

1. A Full Equity Partnership

In this kind of partnership, the money partner funds the full purchase of the property and all repairs (if it is a rehab project). The entrepreneurial partner runs the day-to-day operations required to complete the project. This is often done for smaller deals with a quick exit strategy such as house flipping. The reason why you would purchase the property in full is because these types of properties are usually in very bad shape (thus the need for rehab) and banks and lenders are not likely to fund these properties with mortgages. In such cases, to be able to circumvent that and close quickly and efficiently, the best way is to buy it in full. The great news is that you can pick these properties up for very low prices so it isn't as difficult to purchase in full.

2. A Down Payment Equity Partnership

Mortgages most often require a down payment. Not every potential partner has the full payment needed upfront to pursue a purchase. Nor would you want to pay for every property in full. We want to leverage mortgages as efficiently as possible so long as the numbers still work. Therefore, you can either split the down payment with the money partner or often they can fund the whole amount.

The mortgage can be in either just your partner's name (if you do not have the credit to be able to hold any more mortgages) or under both your names. The division of cash flow and equity in this kind of equity partnership is also based on negotiation but is 50/50 in most cases. A mortgage advisor's recommendations for structuring this type of partnership can be invaluable.

3. A Private Lending Partnership

This partnering strategy relies on the money partner protecting their interest with a lien on the property while the entrepreneurial partner is given free rein in running the project.

For example, Ethan as the partner who has no money but is active in operations, offers his silent partner, William, a solid interest rate on the money he receives for the deal. William, because he trusts

Ethan's reputation as a real estate project manager, decides he will fund 100% of the purchase price and all the costs of renovation. Ethan is pleased that he won't have to seek additional finance and confident the joint venture will proceed well because he has the right skills to get the job done. William is pleased he doesn't have to commit any time to doing the necessary work.

After finishing up, the partnership results in a successful sale for William and Ethan, with William seeing a 12% annual return on his investment or whatever rate was agreed upon. He asks Ethan to find more properties they can invest in together. Ethan is pleased with the partnership too as his excellent management of costs and time-savings throughout the project allow him to grow his business and his reputation.

These individuals that loan money for % interest and NOT equity are also known as private lenders which we will touch on more in depth in the next chapter.

4. Credit Partnership

In a credit partnership, your partner doesn't come up with cash for a down payment if you have and want to use the cash for it. Instead they get a mortgage for the purchase and operations funds are made available to you. These types of partnerships often require less equity or return to the credit partner and more equity for you to keep. Do whatever is fair for both parties. ALWAYS.

For this to work, you need to either have the cash yourself for the down payment or a hard money lender or private lender is approached to finance the purchase and costs of renovation. This type of partnership can work well if the deal is a good one. As well, finding a credit partner, someone who is connected and able to get financing for you can be an asset at every stage in your investment strategy.

It's important to consult with specialists for the best routes to structuring this type of partnership: an attorney for advice on the partnership terms, and a Chartered Professional Accountant (CPA) for the financial structure.

In a credit partnership of this kind, it's helpful to focus on the benefits of the future rewards.

Risks of Joint Venture Agreements

Before continuing with discussing your personal brand and its impact on your potential for successful partnerships, I'd like to briefly touch on some risks of partnerships. In certain circumstance, misunderstandings may occur if the partnership is not properly structured and managed. Some of the key things to watch for are listed below.

---

1. Conflicts of Personality

It can take time to build the right relationship. People have different personalities which can either complement or clash with each other. During a partnership, each person is reliant on the other and if there is a conflict of personality, issues of poor communication may result in a difficult partnership.

2. Differences of Opinion

As individuals, we all have differing views and opinions on a wide variety of topics of interest to us. During partnership, differences of opinion can sometimes get in the way of a project's good progress. A commitment to direct communication and the willingness to compromise are valuable tools for successful partnership.

3. Issues of Trust/Suspicion

No matter who we partner with, there is always a testing of trust and a sense of suspicion if things don't seem to be going well. This is especially true in matters of finance. Delegating the bookkeeping to an unbiased third party can help with maintaining a good balance of trust in a partnership.

4. Delays in Decision Making

Depending on the type of partnership and the role each partner adopts, certain big decisions will need to be made together. And this process is quite different from making decisions alone.

Setting out areas of responsibility for decision-making at the start or deciding whether one partner is primary and the other silent can help smooth the way for good relations through the course of the joint venture. Discuss what will happen during a difference of opinion before it happens.

5. Smaller Profits

In a partnership, profit is shared as agreed and will be smaller than if the venture was undertaken alone. Remembering that the deal would not be possible without your partner's investment and that gaining half of something is better than having nothing helps us put smaller profits in perspective.

6. Mixing Business with Friendship

While it's often said that we shouldn't mix business with pleasure, we may feel that our friends are the best people we can work with because it's our friends who know us better than anyone. And yet, because working together involves both money and time, it's best to expect the unexpected. Have an attorney review your partnership agreement to make sure you're protected if things don't go according to plan.

7. Unrealistic Expectations

Along with excitement at the start of a partnership there can be unrealistic expectations. It's important for both partners to acknowledge that nothing is certain in real estate and that deals are based on educated guesswork.

As the entrepreneurial partner, it's important to provide what you know and prepare for the costs that may arise within the project. In pure lending partnerships, unrealistic expectations are less of an issue as money is borrowed for a fixed term at a fixed interest rate.

8. Legal Responsibility for a Partner

From a business point of view, you are responsible for your partner and vice versa. If one of you skips town without a trace, the other is held responsible. So, it's important to have an attorney draft your partnership agreements, to protect your interests and your financial future.

9. More Complicated Taxes

The more members there are in your business, the more complex you will find your tax season. The bookkeeping also becomes more complex and time-consuming with more members as it costs more to keep it all in order.

Successful Partnerships

As you can see from the above discussion of possible risks and misunderstandings, it's vital that partners communicate well, integrate ideas, provide each other with sufficient support, and iron out potential difficulties before they arise.

Success in a real estate joint venture relies first and foremost on two or more people being in agreement on the aims and objectives of the venture. And this ability for successful partnership in real estate ventures rests almost entirely on your ability to attract partners whose contribution and skills are a good match with your own.

Earlier in this chapter, I mentioned how it's possible to build a reputation and attract the respect of worthy partners in real estate joint ventures. I'd like to cover this now in more detail as it's the number one way to attract money to yourself and your business.

Building an Attractive and Personal Brand

Along with asking yourself questions about the benefits you bring to your interactions with others, remember your brand consists of two things: yourself and your product. Most of all, people buy into you rather than what you are selling.

While establishing yourself as a brand within your community and network, it's helpful to keep your brand message consistent and clear. And to be the best version of you, to have integrity, to be someone people can trust and someone people can believe.

---

1. Your Reputation

As a fragile extension of yourself, your reputation must be handled with great care at all times. This reaches into every aspect of your business and your personal life. And since you're building a creative real estate business, it all matters.

In recognizing that every move you make is observable, and people are watching, remember that people are looking for someone who is serious about success and who will be a worthy investment partner.

2. Your Knowledge

Develop your personal brand through knowledge. Remember never to pretend to know more than you do. Rather make use of the gaps in your knowledge as motivation to grow. Don't be afraid to say, "I don't know the answer to that question, but I will find out and get back to you on it."

Reading is a great way to enhance your knowledge. You can also attend real-estate meet-ups, share with local real-estate investors over a coffee, and listen to podcasts about real estate. Get involved in online forums or gain experience through volunteering under an experienced real estate investor.

3. Your Experience

Strengthen your personal brand through your experience. Building a track record of successful ventures is your greatest ally in establishing your personal brand. A new investor will want to seek out partners who have excellent track records and build shared experiences that create value for others.

4. Your Network

Keep a close proximity to other investors and what you lack in experience can be compensated for through education and building a good network of mentors and visionaries.

Your reputation and your business and brand all have a major impact on your ability to secure joint venture funding. The good news is that the development of these is within your personal control.

Building your Product and Partnerships

An appreciation for your product is a natural consequence of the respect people have for your personal brand.

Real estate is a relationship-building business. As an investor, deciding whether to enter into a partnership for a joint venture or not is your choice. Remember that while you may have a great partner, not every deal will be a great one. Do your due diligence and build a long-lasting relationship with your partner.

Creative financing offers you many opportunities for real estate investing if you have an open mind. And a good partnership can bring life to creative ideas that would otherwise be out of reach.

CHAPTER 8

Hard money and Private lenders

Capitalizing on property using private money, borrowed money not sourced through the traditional mortgage loan institutions or banks, is a creative financial technique to generate financial success with little or no investing of your own funds.

Hard money loans and private lender loans are alternative forms of creative financing that might fit a specific deal or negotiation. Before we charge headlong into the nitty gritty, let's get a firm grasp on the meaning and concept of hard money and private lenders.

Hard money is really just an asset based loan, where the property you are looking to finance is the asset on which the loan is based. These loans are granted by private investors or companies and carry a high interest rate.

The loan is granted based on the viability of the investment potential of the property, and unlike banks and traditional lenders, only a little weight on the credibility of the person securing the loan. With this in mind, hard money loans are attractive because the lender tends to base the loan amount on the after repaired value (ARV) of the financed property. Whereas traditional lending institutions look at the purchase price and not the potential. Hard money lenders project, they look at the worth after the re-pairs and upgrades have been instituted. Hard money lenders usually lend 65 to 70% of the ARV, though I have also found some that do up to 90%. It really depends on your negotiations.

It doesn't matter to the hard money lender whether you are credible in your own right. Should you default on the terms laid down, they simply sell the collateral property and recoup their investment in that way.

Bridge loans have become a well-known phenomenon in the real estate world, and hard money is really just this in a different form. A key distinction between the two is certainly that a hard loan is preferred in cases of default mortgages, arrears, bankruptcies and foreclosures; where bridge loans are common for commercial and investment properties where traditional financing is not yet an option.

Hard money loans are characterized by the short-term nature of the loan, the high interest charged and the speed with which it is processed. The loans also carry a higher than normal number of loan points. A loan point is a fee charged upfront, based on the loan amount. Where traditional mortgage banking institutions charge 1% of the loan amount, hard money lenders will charge considerably more than this. Typically 3% to even 5%.

The loan amount, and the terms of the loan revolve entirely around the value of the property to be financed. Hard money lenders are investors, or groups of investors, who have large sums of money which they are interested in investing to make a high return very quickly. Although not traditional institutional money lenders or property financers, hard money lenders are nonetheless official and licensed money lenders. The property under review should therefore have a high potential to become a viable equity-bearing investment property within a short period of time.

Hard money is obviously expensive, and it requires careful planning and realistic number crunching to turn this expensive option into a real and actual money-making opportunity. Convenience and availability have always been expensive. Why should it be any different when borrowing money?

For ease of comprehension, let's look at a real term scenario comparing a hard money loan with a traditional bank mortgage loan:

We find a commercial building on the market for $1,000,000 and after running some numbers we are excited that this would be a great investment opportunity. Even though it is currently untenanted and therefore not bringing in a ready income, once we've done a bit of work on the building and put a reliable management company in charge, it will make us a good return. Here's the problem though, we only have $500,000. Because the property is not currently bringing in an income, we will not be considered eligible for a traditional loan from a bank or lending institution, and we don't know of anyone in our circle or family who has that kind of money, who could fund us.

Fortunately, we have the option of hard money lenders. We approach just such an investor and prove the potential investment value of the property. He is willing to put down the money needed, subject to certain terms. For his $500 000 loan, he wants $30 000 upfront and imposes a 12% interest rate. He is willing to set a 2-year term to the loan, meaning he wants all the money paid back within 2 years.

This sounds a little steep compared with the traditional mortgage loan route. However, once the building is tenanted and bringing in its full potential in rentals, and we have refinanced it, it will make a decent return. This is why investors use hard money loans, even though they have high interest rates and very steep upfront payments, they have the potential to buy the property and make a significant profit on it. Without the hard money, the option to buy the building would not be there.

	Traditional Lender	Hard Money Lender
Loan Amount	$500 000	$500 000
Interest	6%	12%
Loan Point/Upfront	1.5 points / $7500	6 points / $30000
Loan Term	10 – 15 years	0.5 - 1 Year
Funds available	1 month	2 weeks

Use hard money to finance flips and fixer uppers or to fund rental properties until they are viable for long term financing. Let's look at another scenario to get a better idea of how this works:

You find a fixer-upper from a motivated seller for $60 000 needing $30,000 in renovations, it's after repairs value (ARV) is $130,000. Hard money lenders typically show a willingness to lend 65% to 75% of the ARV. Your lender is prepared to finance 70% of the ARV, being $91 000, and requires tenders on the envisaged upgrades and construction. The terms set out are 15% interest and 4 loan points. The lender then hands over 25% on the closing of the deal. Increments of 25% are subsequently handed over as the repairs are completed. Interest is not charged and neither is the loan point amount, until the house has been sold, at which point the lender will expect the loan capital, points and interest to be paid in one large amount. Based on a loan period of 6 months this will be what you're looking at cost-wise: the interest payable amounts to $6,825, and the points come in at $3,640. You're paying back $101,465. The lender has pocketed over $10 000 on a 6-month loan. You have potentially made $28 535 in six months. Subtract any legal, closing and sales costs safely estimated at about 10% or $13,000 and you get a net profit of $15,535. Not too shabby for 6 months. Now imagine if you are doing 10+ flips per year which is not unrealistic. I know a lot of people who flip 10+ properties even on their first year! Once you have a system in place, the right education, are involved with a great network and have great mentorship and guidance, the sky is the limit!

The fact that you were able to make an offer on a potentially great investment property without having to wait on bank approval means you could purchase the property in the first place. This is the benefit of hard money. Knowing you have ready investors to back the real estate deals when they crop up.

Having explained hard money and used various scenarios to paint a picture of how these lenders work, let's now get an idea of what a private lender is and how they differ from hard money lenders.

A private lender is a non-bank, it could be a business acquaintance, friend or family member or accredited investors unknown to you personally, who loans money for property funding undertakings. The private lender bases his loan on the viability of the property being financed and also on the credibility of the person taking out the loan, although less so than traditional bank lenders, but more than a HML.

Private money loans characteristically offer three term ranges: Typically, short term loans are six months to two years, and used for flipping real estate or refinancing. Medium term is between two and ten years, and is commonly used on fixer uppers for leasing as well as refinancing or other those deals where the cash isn't tied up for long periods. Long term is over ten years, and is typically for buy and holds.

While they are similar to hard money lenders in as much as their loans are asset based at higher interest rates over a short loan period, they do have marked differences. Their rates are generally lower than a HML. In my experience, private lenders loan anywhere from 5% to 12% whereas HML loan at 12% to 18%.

Flexibility is the key difference here. Since the private lender is not in it professionally, as a vested means of earning an income, private lending becomes more of a relationship than hard money dealings are. The terms of the borrowed money are entirely negotiable. Since private money has no pre-set criteria or possible middle men to appease, the loan term, interest charged and limits applied are open to modification. As long as both the lender and borrower are happy, the deal is on. You are more in charge of the money you receive from private lenders, than you would be with hard money.

Limits on lending, interest rates, and loan duration are all, as they say, on the table for discussion, so a simple commitment to an agreement suitable to all parties will often get the job done. This also makes hard money a more expensive route than private money, for the most part.

Hard money is easier to come by, since hard money lenders tend to advertise the availability of loans, being that they are in the business of making a profit from monies which they have access to, be it their own, as part of an investor group or from third party sources. Private money, as denoted by the term, are private entities who have the funds and are willing to lend it for investment purposes. So, how would one get in contact with a private lender, if the need arose?

Finding viable real estate is one thing, funding it requires a whole other set of skills. Unfortunately, an eye for a good deal is not the be-all and end-all of a smart property investor. The particular set of skills needed to ensure that the required money is readily available when the deal presents itself is invaluable. This being said, let's go back to our scenario.

That $1,000,000 commercial property you bought, knowing you only have $500,000 to contribute, would not have been possible without having a known investor. Knowing that a traditional lending institution wouldn't see it as a credible property because it wasn't bringing in a ready income, you still had hard money and private money to choose from. Had you put in the time and effort networking, you might have saved the high cost of securing the hard money by going with a cheaper private lender.

Fortunately, you have spent the last year hard at work networking and building up a ready source of private money lenders. Friends and family members who are suitably liquid to have the money to invest, are your easiest and, typically, the most popular option. The downside of this option is the risk of damaging relationships should an investment not turn out as well as expected, or should it quite simply sink entirely. Taking loans from sources who are not professionally equipped to see the viability of the investment property, or the lack of viability more importantly, may prove disadvantageous.

But don't be discouraged, to be a successful property investor you need to put in the time and effort. By making valuable connections with friends and colleagues of your friends and family, you can land beneficial investors. Network at parties, at functions and at social gatherings. You never know who might be there looking for a way to earn additional income from their available resources, unless you speak about your real estate business. Obviously, you will need to put more work into accessing these investors, as they won't be as ready to hand over their money as your friends and family might. Presentations and proposals are needed to build up a trusting and transparent business relationship.

Potential investors are available if you know where to look, and you can find investors who are not personal acquaintances by accessing investor contact sites. These investors will take longer to convert to capital partners, which is why we say creative financing takes time and effort.

Hard money and private lenders can be valuable strategies to finding the right creative financing techniques for your situation. Using this or one of the other steps to become financially successful without investing much money is now well within your grasp.

Make a Million Dollars

The whole idea behind the techniques described in this book is about creating financial abundance and accessing freedom through real estate. There might be parts of the book you want to reread or connect deeper with. As you get ready to take action it is my hope that you have become aware about which creative financing option works best for you. So, now that you have all of this information, knowledge is no longer the problem. You need to find the right solution. Before we go, I want you to make a commitment towards taking action, and I highly recommend finding a mentor. Through networking events and finding what is available in your jurisdiction, you will quickly learn who to talk to, how to get started and where the best mentors are sharing their experience. Nothing will take place if you don't take action.

As well, let's talk about really creating wealth, the main reason most of us are getting into the real estate industry. The dream of creating a million dollars is a spark but how to make it a reality? Following the tricks and tips in this book will get you well on your way. You want to create a million dollars in real estate and you are ready to take action. We've shown you techniques that you could do. Now I will add in a dash of the secret spice that made it possible to grow that financial abundance.

This is the part where we can really get excited. Now you have all the steps laid out, including options that are often misunderstood or discouraged by traditional professionals. The way to become a millionaire through real estate is so simple. It's already outlined in this one book. That's how simple it is.

Here's the big kicker though, and here's what people don't tell you. Everyone tells you, "It's easy, it's easy, it's easy, just do this, just take action." Guess what? It's simple, but it's not easy, and there is a big difference between something being simple and easy.

It's simple because all you have to do is follow a time-tested, proven formula and system, which is already outlined in this book, and can also be found online, in other real estate courses or other books. A system is a system and if you follow it correctly, it's simple. It'll get you from A to B, if you follow the system, and it's just that simple.

Is it going to be easy? Now, this part is what really, really depends on you. You can make it difficult for yourself by overcomplicating, by never taking action and always doubting or backing out at the last minute. You can have a negative mindset. Making mistakes happens, the important thing is knowing what to do when you screw up. People who do not succeed are the ones who make it as difficult for themselves as possible. There are ways of making it easier on yourself but it takes work and you must be willing to put in the time. There's no way of getting around. Even though we want to work smart and not work hard that is not to imply that you're not working at all.

The secret spice is hustle; you have to put in the work. You have to put in that commitment to constant hard work now or preferably yesterday. You have to get out of your comfort zone and start finding deals that best fit your intentions. 90% of real estate is networking and building relationships with people. 10% of the time actually involves negotiations and making deals. Why? Because it revolves around so much of in the creation of a deal that is a win/win for everyone involved. The saying that your network is your net worth, that really shines through so much in the real estate industry.

You can't just be by yourself and not know anything and not interact with other investors, or go to real estate events or a real estate association around your locality or anything like that. It is not possible. Instead, you have to be willing to get and stay involved in that circle. It takes dedication and you have to go and network with other like-minded people, potential investors and sellers in your area or other people globally through the Internet. That's the beauty of the Internet, we can connect with like-minded people on a global scale.

We might live in a tiny town with a lot of closed-minded people, but the beauty is, you can still connect with like-minded entrepreneurs or investors like yourself, by using the power of the Internet. There's no excuse to not being able to network and put you self out there and connect with other people that are experienced innovators as well as investors in the real estate industry.

It's not just real estate, it's whatever industry you're in, you have to be involved in that community. It's really important to network. How can you find investors? How can you learn about new techniques? How can you keep up with current affairs, and different techniques that people are doing that are working for them, if you're not involved with the community?

A lot of times when you explain your plans for one of these creative strategies to a mortgage broker or a bank or a lender they'll be quite expressive and tell you, "What are you talking about? That's never going to work." Even though that's what you'll hear most of the time from traditional agencies, I am telling you that it does work, and you can do this. The thing is most lenders or even mortgage brokers, they don't know anything about creative finance. They don't know how to structure it and they'll automatically tell you that that's never going to work, but it's absolutely not true. If you don't have a mentor to work with through the first few deals, you might read it in this book and you go to your mortgage broker. Once they have said no, most people stop after that.

Whereas, if you have a mentor or somebody that you can refer to, you can go back to them and say, "Hey, I went to my mortgage broker. They told me that lease options don't work, or it's illegal." Then your mentor can step in because they have done it before. If your mortgage broker doesn't know what they're talking about, your mentor can send you to their mortgage broker or provide other steps so that you are successful. This is why it is so important to find a coach or mentor that has ALREADY DONE what you want to do! They've already made the mistakes and proven that it is possible to do. There is absolutely no reason why you can't do it too especially with their guidance!

It's about how you structure this whole thing. Sometimes as deals require it, you might need to work with different people, because not everybody, even lenders and brokers, knows how to implement these strategies. Not everybody will know this information, and regular realtors might, in some circumstances, be the most closed-minded. You want to deal with investor-friendly realtors, because regular realtors, will likely try to sell you a home as a personal home.

The thing is, you're not buying a personal home, you're buying an investment property. It's completely different, from the things that you want to be looking for to the things that your realtor should be showing you. The same thing can be said for your mortgage broker. It should be an investor-friendly mortgage broker. In the beginning, it takes time to differentiate who to put on your team, as it were.

That's why networking is very, very important. That's definitely probably the biggest thing that anyone, anywhere can take action on right now. Start getting involved in local real estate communities and associations. Look for mentors and coaches, connect to people who can answer your questions and guide you through your uncertainties. Look up some potential meetings and events in your area or contact me for help at **nicosanchez.ca**.

By getting involved in communities like Team Made Real Estate, everyone begins to share their skills and work towards the greater good. Give it a try and start going to real estate seminars and events, and networking galas and stuff like that. If you want to be successful, really get yourself into that community, because that's how you're going to learn more, and that's how you're going to continue to grow.

The key is a mindset. How do you earn a million dollars in real estate? The answer to that question is it's through leveraging, and remaining confidently optimistic. It's not like you're going to make a million dollars on one deal, but it's about the formula. It's about focus, right? The formula for success can be different depending on each person's specific needs. Once you figure out a formula that works, whether it be joint venture, private lender or other creative financing, you just have to now duplicate it, leverage it. If you were able to do one deal every quarter in the year, that would be four times the returns.

As you do the math you can see how this can bloom into something remarkable in a short period of time. Now, you will always aim for growth so if you did four deals, in one year, the next one you will do more. The next year, you work towards a goal of eight deals, and that's how you can earn one million dollars.

Of course, this is just a guide and it depends on your goals and anything else going on in your life. You can do it as fast as you want, or as slow as you want, but you can definitely follow the system and work your way to get to million dollars. It becomes a bit of a challenge and as you get going, the million-dollar deal is a big goal. Breaking it down though, it's just learning the four ways you build your wealth in real estate. It's the cash flow, the appreciation, the equity pay-down, and the tax benefits. With even the first three alone, the cash flow, appreciation and equity pay-down, once you have a certain number of properties it can be possible to achieve that large goal in one year.

Doing it more slowly is definitely possible and some would say less risky as you have time to find the deals that are sure to succeed. That being said, you can hit a million dollars' net worth in one year which I have personally been able to do, using creativity over capital. It's as simple as that. You can take as long as you want to achieve that, don't get me wrong, I am not encouraging anyone to rush into things blindly. What it comes down to is that you can use any of these strategies to get your first deal. And, the first paves the way and provides equity for a system of real estate investments that add up fast.

It all depends on what type of hustle you've got. It all depends on how bad you want it. It depends on how much action you're taking. It depends on your drive and your motivation, and it just depends on you. It's as simple as not allowing ourselves to blame other people, or our situation. If we stop blaming the government and blaming our parents and our friends we can begin to take responsibility for ourselves. You are in control of everything that happens to you.

It's really true, you can control what you want in your future. When it comes down to it, each individual has to take action in order for these systems to work.

As a final example, I want to show you the difference that a mentor can make in the investment decisions you make. Through trial and error, you will learn on your own but with help, you can lose a lot less in the process. This is zero down real estate at it's finest. Here's what the gurus don't tell you. In this example, you have $100,000 in the bank. Now would you choose to use the $100,000 to pay 100K, all cash for one property? Or would you use 25% to buy four properties with that same amount? The options of course are endless and a mentor or someone who has made the choice time and again might show you that you can use 10% of that $100,000 and buy 10 properties with that. For example, you might be able to get 15% vendor take-back so rather than needing to put 25% for the down payment you only need to put 10%. With the same $100,000 you can purchase 10 of these properties. Now you are making cashflow and building equity on 10x properties rather than just ONE! If you were speaking to me, I might explain that I prefer to use zero down, and that way I can buy unlimited properties with that. Do you see now how you can scale much larger and faster with just a little creativity? Rather than using $100,000 to buy 1 paid in full, or 4 with 25% down or 10 at 10% down, you can acquire an unlimited amount. Time and money isn't what is holding you back, it's you, your mindset and your creativity! At the same time, I would show you how the equity and cash flow would change depending on which way you decide to invest.

The intent here, as I promised at the beginning of the book, is to show you how it can be done. This is just the beginning and I encourage everyone to continue to learn, and seek out alternative sources of advice. Seek coaches and mentors and make sure to network with the right people. Doing that will drive you to action and help overcome that fear. As well, you will be forced to discuss the intricacies of the techniques, learning to constantly remember to be aware of your mindset.

The actual techniques, become bullet points to success which is exactly how to get started. At this point, after you have furthered your training and knowledge. Getting coaching and mentorship opens the doors for opportunities to network with the right types of people, then the mindset is an afterthought because it is so engrained into your action taking habits. As you work with these people more and more, you will start to know exactly what you are doing and how to build upon that to form an impressive portfolio. Not only that, but it becomes possible to figure out how to design deals that fit your requirements. Learning that gives you something to build on and build up and know exactly what steps are required. For me I learned exactly what I did wrong because I had advisors to go to the last couple times when I did fail.

Up until the point where I actually took the cours-es for the education that I got for real estate, and up until I had actual mentorship and actual coaching, I was always unsure of what I was doing until I had an actual coach and a mentor, that I could refer back to. Every time I was stuck on a deal, I would literally refer back to my coach and my mentor and ask for help by telling them, "I'm stuck on this part," or "Here are the numbers," or "This is what's happen-ing right now. What should I do? Should I go for-ward? Is this a good position to be in? Is this a bad position to be in?"

It made a big difference when I had that help, that reassurance, from somebody that's done it before. I have that encouragement from them saying, "Yes, that's good, go ahead with it," or "No, that's not good, do something else," or "pull out" or "look at another property, or maybe try it this other way, try to structure a deal this other way." Just having that mentorship and the coaching, somebody that I could constantly refer to every time that I was stuck, prevented me from making costly mistakes. That is what took out the rest of the fear that I had.

When you have reached the point where you've already overcome your fear, that is the point where you'd be ready and able to take action. What are you afraid of, though? Literally nothing; you can't be afraid of anything when you have all the basic and technical knowledge, and you also have somebody who's done it before to now reassure you that you're either doing it right or you're doing it wrong. There's no more fear at that point, and you can really now pull the trigger. You can be sure that these techniques work, and you can learn how the will work for you.

As you begin to make plans, for your own investments, ready to jump in and take action, you might think about starting off with friends and family. Often there are people in our lives, maybe an uncle is a doctor or other busy professional who knows the value of real estate and knows that they can get more return in real estate as an investment. It's now up to you to show them and give them a presentation. This is the investor proposal. Actually, I have a template you can use and simply insert your information. That brings you one step closer to taking action. If you want my investor proposal template visit **nicosanchez.ca/bonus**. There you will also find a few other templates and resources including the credibility builder and joint venture agreement. Some of these documents can be quite pricy to have drafted, which is another benefit of working with a network of knowledgeable mentors; you can all share the wealth.

We have gone through some quite technical information so keep this as a guide or refer to the resources provided to see you through as you take action. Dare to be the 1% who gathers the knowledge and uses it to build a life with more financial freedom. Too many people don't have the confidence to get started. Use the information contained herein to make it easier on yourself and find others who have the same goals as you. Now get out there, get creative and get a deal started.

ABOUT THE AUTHOR

Nico is the co-founder and President of DS Realty Solutions Ltd. and President of The Greater Than Group, a Multi Divisional Private Equity Real Estate Investment Company that provides valued investors with great returns on their hands-off investments secured by real estate. With an in-house property management team and construction and renovation company, the Greater Than Group truly provides a one stop shop for your real estate investment needs.

He is now also an acclaimed real estate investment coach, mentor and motivational speaker for Team

Made Real Estate, Canada's top Real Estate Investment Education and Events company.

If you are interested in learning how to take your real estate investing to the next level and would like to work directly with Nico and his team, you may contact him at the link below:

http://www.teammaderealestate.com

Furthermore, he is the Executive Director with The Worldwide Expedition for Peace and Truth Project, Inc. (WEPT), a Non-Profit Organization whose project subscribes to sustainable philanthropy. To learn more about his humanitarian missions check out the WEPT website below!

http://www.theweptproject.com

Nico's Mission and Vision is to help you create wealth through strategic real estate investments and to spearhead humanitarian campaigns worldwide and to motivate, inspire and drive others to achieve more!